POSTWAR AMERICA
WATERGATE

by Nick Rebman

WWW.FOCUSREADERS.COM

Copyright © 2024 by Focus Readers®, Mendota Heights, MN 55120. All rights reserved. No part of this book may be reproduced or utilized in any form or by any means without written permission from the publisher.

Focus Readers is distributed by North Star Editions:
sales@northstareditions.com | 888-417-0195

Produced for Focus Readers by Red Line Editorial.

Content Consultant: Richard M. Filipink Jr., PhD, Professor of History, Western Illinois University

Photographs ©: Charles Tasnadi/AP Images, cover, 1; Corbis Historical/Getty Images, 4–5; Shutterstock Images, 6, 22; Bob Schutz/AP Images, 9; Ollie Noonan/AP Images, 10–11; AP Images, 12, 15, 17, 18–19, 27; Bettmann/Getty Images, 21; Charles W. Harrity/AP Images, 24–25; Red Line Editorial, 29

Library of Congress Cataloging-in-Publication Data
Names: Rebman, Nick, author.
Title: Watergate / by Nick Rebman.
Description: Mendota Heights, MN : Focus Readers, [2024] | Series: Postwar America | Includes bibliographical references and index. | Audience: Grades 4-6
Identifiers: LCCN 2023033124 (print) | LCCN 2023033125 (ebook) | ISBN 9798889980452 (hardcover) | ISBN 9798889980889 (paperback) | ISBN 9798889981695 (ebook pdf) | ISBN 9798889981312 (ebook other)
Subjects: LCSH: Watergate Affair, 1972-1974--Juvenile literature. | Nixon, Richard M. (Richard Milhous), 1913-1994--Juvenile literature. | United States--Politics and government--1969-1974--Juvenile literature.
Classification: LCC E860 .R44 2024 (print) | LCC E860 (ebook) | DDC 973.924--dc23/eng/20230803
LC record available at https://lccn.loc.gov/2023033124
LC ebook record available at https://lccn.loc.gov/2023033125

Printed in the United States of America
Mankato, MN
012024

ABOUT THE AUTHOR
Nick Rebman is a writer and editor who lives in Minnesota.

TABLE OF CONTENTS

CHAPTER 1
Break-In 5

CHAPTER 2
Investigation 11

VOICES FROM THE PAST
Secret Source 16

CHAPTER 3
Hearings 19

CHAPTER 4
Resignation 25

Focus on Watergate • 30
Glossary • 31
To Learn More • 32
Index • 32

CHAPTER 1

BREAK-IN

In 1972, President Richard Nixon was running for re-election. He ran against Senator George McGovern. Nixon was a Republican. McGovern was a Democrat.

The Democratic Party had an office in Washington, DC. The office was in a group of buildings called the Watergate complex. On June 17, 1972, five burglars

President Nixon greets supporters at a parade during his re-election campaign.

 The first Watergate building opened in 1965.

broke in. The police caught them. All five burglars were arrested.

The burglars were carrying cameras. They also had electronic listening devices. The police realized it was not a

6

regular break-in. So, the Federal Bureau of **Investigation** (FBI) got involved. This government group deals with serious crimes.

The FBI soon learned that one of the burglars had ties to Nixon. The burglar worked for the Committee to Re-elect the

AN EARLIER BREAK-IN

The burglars had broken into the Democratic Party's office before. In May 1972, they secretly put listening devices in two telephones. That time, the burglars didn't get caught. But one of the devices wasn't working. So, on June 17, the burglars broke in again. They wanted to replace it. That was when police arrested them.

President (CRP). FBI agents wanted to figure out who had ordered the break-in. They thought the CRP might have done it.

Nixon didn't know about the break-in ahead of time. But a few days later, he found out. He learned that people on his staff were involved. Nixon did not want the public to find out. He feared this news would hurt his chances in the election.

On June 23, Nixon spoke to an **aide**. The aide urged Nixon to secretly block the FBI's investigation. That way, the public would not know who had ordered the break-in. Nixon agreed to this plan. However, blocking an investigation is a crime. It is called obstruction of justice.

President Nixon felt very suspicious of his political opponents.

CHAPTER 2

INVESTIGATION

At first, the Watergate break-in did not get much news coverage. The Vietnam War (1954–1975) was going on at the time. It was a much bigger story. However, a few reporters kept looking into the break-in. Bob Woodward and Carl Bernstein worked for the *Washington Post*. They wrote several articles about

Nixon slowly removed US soldiers from Vietnam. In 1972, US forces were still fighting there.

 Nixon's team pressured some news outlets not to report on Watergate during his campaign.

Watergate. In August 1972, they reported that Nixon's team had paid one of the burglars $25,000.

Nixon spoke to the press. He claimed his staff had not been involved. But

Woodward and Bernstein thought Nixon was lying. So, they kept investigating. In October, they reported that the break-in was part of a bigger plan. Nixon's team was spying on many Democrats.

Nixon and his staff said the reporters were **biased**. Many people believed Nixon. Also, few other reporters were covering Watergate. So, the story did not receive major attention. In November 1972, Nixon won re-election.

The five burglars were charged with crimes. Two other men had helped plan the break-in. They were also charged. By January 1973, all seven men had been found guilty. However, the judge thought they were not telling the whole truth. He believed there was more to the story. The judge said he wanted the men to tell what they knew. He threatened them with long prison sentences.

In March, one of the burglars wrote to the judge. The burglar admitted that he

1972 ELECTION

Nixon won the 1972 election easily. He had one of the biggest wins in US history. He won in 49 of the 50 states. He got nearly 61 percent of the vote. McGovern got less than 38 percent. Nixon's party also did well in the House of Representatives. Democrats still controlled Congress. But Republicans gained 12 seats.

John J. Sirica was the judge in charge of the burglars' trials.

had been told to lie in court. He also said government officials had been involved in the break-in.

VOICES FROM THE PAST

SECRET SOURCE

Bob Woodward and Carl Bernstein had a secret source. The source gave them information. They used this information for their reports. The source was a government official. He met with Woodward in a parking garage. That way, no one would see them. The source "was willing to help and guide us," Woodward explained. For example, Woodward said the source talked about "some sort of connection to the White House."[1]

The source told Woodward not to use his real name. He knew he could lose his job for sharing secrets. So, Woodward used a nickname. He called the source "Deep Throat."

Deep Throat's real name stayed a mystery for many years. But in 2005, someone came forward. Mark Felt admitted that he was the source. Felt had been high up in the FBI. He was angry when

Bernstein (left) and Woodward (right) helped the *Washington Post* win the Pulitzer Prize in 1973.

Nixon's team tried to block the FBI's investigation. He believed the truth needed to come out.

In 2008, Woodward talked about Felt. He explained the most important thing he learned. "Watergate was not isolated," Woodward said. Instead, "it was a part of a series of secret activities to spy on Democrats."[2]

1. "Woodward: Deep Throat a man of courage." *NPR*. NPR, 19 Dec. 2008. Web. 5 Apr. 2023.
2. Ibid.

17

CHAPTER 3

HEARINGS

Many lawmakers were concerned about the Watergate break-in. They wanted to find out who had ordered it. So, the US Senate created a group to investigate. Senators asked Nixon's aides to **testify**. At first, Nixon would not let them. He claimed executive privilege. This allows the president to keep some things secret.

Seven senators were part of the Senate Watergate Committee. They held hearings about the scandal.

Hearings began in May 1973. They went on for months. Eventually, many people on Nixon's staff agreed to testify. Nixon's former lawyer spoke to the Senate in June. He said Nixon had blocked the FBI's investigation. Nixon denied it. Then in July, one of Nixon's aides testified. He said Nixon's conversations had been secretly recorded.

In October, a **special prosecutor** told Nixon to hand over the recordings. Nixon refused. Once again, he claimed executive privilege. Nixon also had the special prosecutor fired. Two high-level officials disagreed with Nixon's decision. So, they quit their jobs.

The special prosecutor was Archibald Cox (left).

Nixon came under heavy pressure. Many lawmakers said he had misused his power. Finally, Nixon agreed to release some recordings. One was from April 1973. It showed Nixon was trying to avoid telling the truth about Watergate.

The House of Representatives began different hearings in May 1974. House

The Supreme Court decides cases from their building in Washington, DC.

members were deciding whether to impeach Nixon. Impeachment is when the House charges someone with a crime. The process can take months.

In July, the Supreme Court made a ruling. Every justice agreed. The ruling said Nixon had to hand over the rest of the recordings. In early August, he gave them to the new special prosecutor and Congress. One recording was from June 1972. It proved that Nixon had blocked the FBI's investigation.

EXECUTIVE PRIVILEGE

The Supreme Court ruled that executive privilege is allowed in certain cases. For example, some information could put the nation in danger. The president does not need to share it. However, that did not apply to Nixon. So, he had to hand over the recordings. Many presidents have used executive privilege. But some experts believe it should not exist. They say the US Constitution does not mention it.

CHAPTER 4

RESIGNATION

The release of the recordings had a huge impact. Nixon knew his career was over. He knew the House would impeach him. And he knew the Senate would remove him from office. Nixon did not want to go through this process. So, in August 1974, he **resigned**. He became the first US president to do so.

Nixon announced his resignation on August 8, 1974. He left the White House the next day.

Nixon was never charged with a crime. But many people on his staff were. More than 30 people were found guilty for their roles in the **scandal**. Most were not part of the break-in. They had helped with the cover-up.

A NEW PRESIDENT

Spiro Agnew was Nixon's first vice president. However, Agnew was involved in a different scandal. He had accepted bribes. So, he resigned in October 1973. Nixon chose Gerald Ford as the new vice president. Ford became president when Nixon resigned. Ford then **pardoned** Nixon. That meant Nixon could not be charged for his role in Watergate. Many people disagreed with Ford's decision. They thought Nixon should have gone on trial.

President Ford faced many challenges when he took office. Regaining the nation's trust was one.

After Watergate, Congress passed many new laws. Lawmakers hoped these rules would stop similar scandals from happening. One law had to do with election spending. Another law tried to limit the president's power.

Watergate affected reporting, too. For example, Woodward and Bernstein inspired many other reporters. More newspapers started doing deep investigations. Reporters also started treating politicians differently. Fewer reporters believed that politicians were telling the truth.

Watergate also had a major effect on the public. People had less faith in their leaders. In the mid-1960s, more than 75 percent of Americans had trusted the government. But after Watergate, the number fell to 36 percent. By the early 2020s, it was down to 20 percent. Watergate was not the only cause of this drop. But in many ways, Watergate marked the beginning of the modern era of politics.

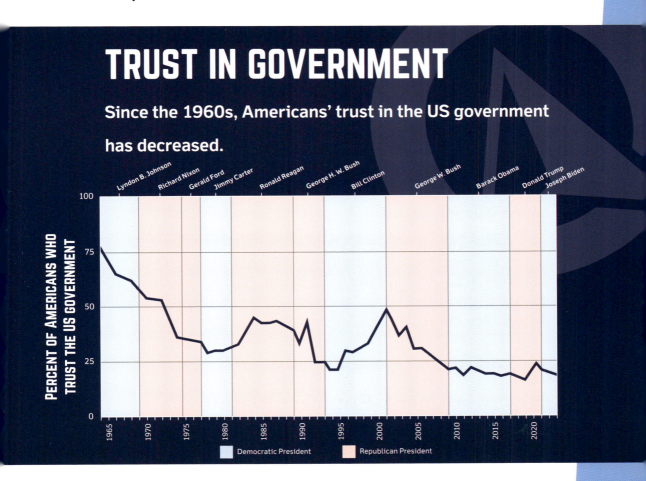

FOCUS ON WATERGATE

Write your answers on a separate piece of paper.

1. Write a paragraph explaining the main idea of Chapter 3.

2. Do you think reporters should trust government officials? Why or why not?

3. When did the Senate hearings begin?
    - **A.** June 1972
    - **B.** May 1973
    - **C.** August 1974

4. Why did Nixon's team pay burglars to break into the Watergate building?
    - **A.** They hoped to impeach President Nixon.
    - **B.** They hoped to learn the Democrats' secrets.
    - **C.** They hoped to destroy the Democrats' office.

Answer key on page 32.

GLOSSARY

aide
A person who helps someone do a job.

biased
Had unfair beliefs about a certain person or group.

hearings
Meetings in which lawmakers ask questions and gather information.

investigation
A detailed attempt to learn the truth about something.

pardoned
Officially decided that someone does not have to face the consequences of a crime they committed.

resigned
Gave up a position or quit a job.

scandal
An event that many people find shocking or disgraceful.

special prosecutor
A lawyer from outside the government who investigates a case.

testify
To speak in court.

TO LEARN MORE

BOOKS

Britton, Tamara L. *Richard Nixon*. Minneapolis: Abdo Publishing, 2021.

Francis, Sandra. *Gerald R. Ford*. Mankato, MN: The Child's World, 2020.

Krasner, Barbara. *Exploring the Executive Branch*. Minneapolis: Lerner Publications, 2020.

NOTE TO EDUCATORS

Visit **www.focusreaders.com** to find lesson plans, activities, links, and other resources related to this title.

INDEX

Bernstein, Carl, 11, 13, 16, 28
burglars, 5–7, 12–14

Democrats, 5, 7, 13–14, 17

Federal Bureau of Investigation (FBI), 7–8, 16–17, 20, 23
Felt, Mark, 16–17
Ford, Gerald, 26, 29

hearings, 20–21
House of Representatives, 14, 21–22, 25

impeach, 22, 25

listening devices, 6–7

obstruction of justice, 8

pardon, 26

recordings, 20–21, 23, 25
resign, 25–26

Supreme Court, 22–23

US Senate, 19–20, 25

Woodward, Bob, 11, 13, 16–17, 28

Answer Key: **1.** Answers will vary; **2.** Answers will vary; **3.** B; **4.** B

32